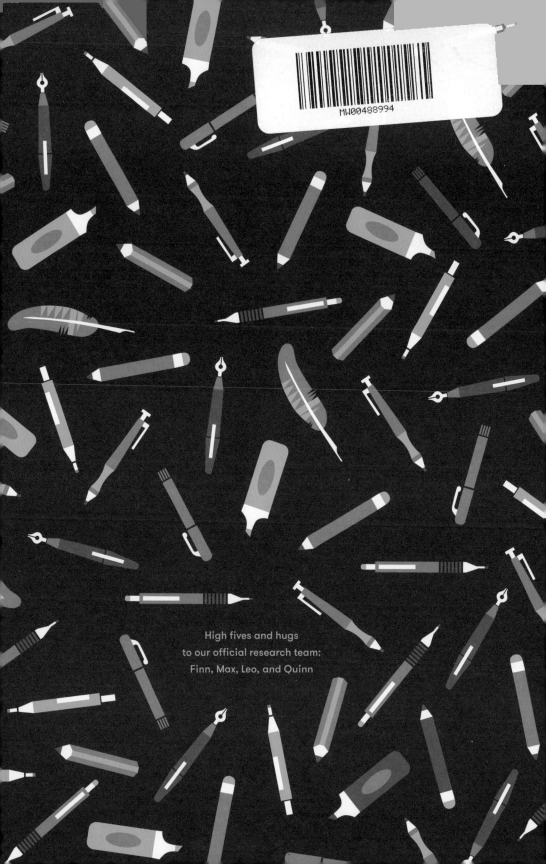

High fives and hugs
to our official research team:
Finn, Max, Leo, and Quinn

What's this book about?

This is a place for your stories—narratives, poems, comics, song lyrics—true ones, made-up ones, and are-you-kidding-me ridiculous ones.

This journal has a bunch of tips and prompts to get your creative juices flowing. There's lots of space for writing, but not nearly enough; so keep some extra paper handy.

Ready? Write On...

Stories by:

....

Dedicated to:

....

because:

....

....

About the Author

your portrait

your name

_____ ,

from _____ ,

hometown

is [age] years old, and

goes to _____ .

your school

[handwritten: Kayla]

prefers to write with a:

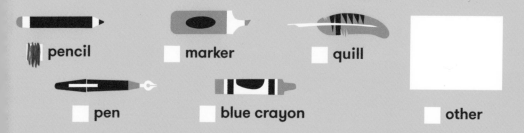

☐ pencil ☐ marker ☐ quill

☐ pen ☐ blue crayon ☐ other

and is most inspired by

[handwritten] .

If _[handwritten: Kayne]_ **could be**

a character from any book,

it would be _[handwritten]_ .

[handwritten: Kayle] **plans to be a**

[handwritten] **someday.**

What's in a Name?

What's the story behind your name?
If you're not sure, ask around. And if you can't
find out, make up something fantastic.

Hello
my name is

It comes from

Arabic or Hebrew

meaning laurel or

I think it's interesting that

My name Minus ....

5s and Maid things. ....

....

How I feel about my name:

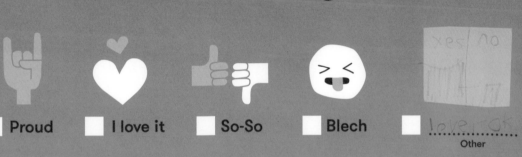

Proud ☐ **I love it** ☐ **So-So** ☐ **Blech** ☐ love it
Other

It might be fun to change my name to

....

This would be my new signature:

Describe It.

The best stories come to life with vivid descriptions. How would you describe these things?

Tip:

Check a thesaurus if you find yourself coming up with the same descriptive words.

For example, this guy is...

An emerald green, tremendously shy, sort of silly turtle.

This cat is...

....

....

....

This submarine is...

....

....

....

This tree is...

....

....

....

....

More descriptions...

This robot is...

....

....

....

This fish is...

....

....

....

This gem is...

....

....

....

This car is...

....

....

....

Such a Character!

You'll want to come up with some interesting characters for your stories. Like a...

A bear with a toothache

A top-secret spy dog

A lost alien

A seriously spunky fairy

Create your own characters, including some details that make them memorable.

This is:

who is very:

and also:

This is:

who is very:

and also:

What's Your Hook?

Great stories start with an attention-grabber. For example, in a story about jellyfish, is it more interesting to start with: *Jellyfish live in the ocean,* or *Did you know that jellyfish poop from their mouths?* (Eww!) A good hook might be a question, or a fascinating fact, or an exclamation.

Come up with some good "hooks" for the following story topics:

Seymour Spider's Amazing Adventure

That Time I Turned Invisible

Jezebel's First Day of Third Grade

Fill in the

Blanks

boy's name	animal

noun	adjective

activity	adverb

Now fill in the words you selected above into this story, and read this strange tale you helped create.

A gnome named [boy's name]

was skipping through the forest when

suddenly a(n) [animal]

jumped out from behind a [noun] .

"Oh!" said the gnome. "You're

very [adjective] .Would you

like to join me for [activity] ?"

The [animal] laughed.

"No one has ever asked me that

before. YES!" And the two

ran [adverb] through

the forest.

The End.

Wee Story Cards

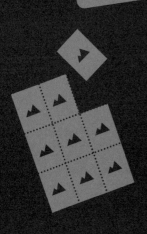

Punch out all
the story cards.

Make three piles
(one of each color).

Pick one card from each pi
and make up a story
based on that scene,
character(s), and conflict

Come up with your own resolution!

It's even more fun if you do it with a friend—
take turns coming up with the silliest stories you can imagine.

Your turn Create your own story cards

SCENE

100 years in the future

SCENE

Just outside a volcano

SCENE

In a pickle factory

SCENE

Inside a really big refrigerator

SCENE

A hidden forest

SCENE

A fish market in Tokyo

SCENE

Deep in the ocean

SCENE

A dance party in outer space

SCENE

Somewhere in Antarctica

SCENE

SCENE

SCENE

CHARACTER

A talking
burrito
and taco

CHARACTER

Fairies
who are
sisters

CHARACTER

Two
aging
robots

CHARACTER

A
relatively
shy whale

CHARACTER

A monster
named
Melville

CHARACTER

A
hilarious
hedgehog

CHARACTER

Nine-
year-old
spies

CHARACTER

Bigfoot

CHARACTER

Three
best
friends

CHARACTER

CHARACTER

CHARACTER

CONFLICT

A dragon swooped in

CONFLICT

Everything grew 20x its size

CONFLICT

They couldn't stop dancing

CONFLICT

Horrible, terrible, bad breath

CONFLICT

Got completely lost

CONFLICT

Sudden darkness

CONFLICT

It started hailing basketballs

CONFLICT

There was zero gravity

CONFLICT

They became invisible

CONFLICT

CONFLICT

CONFLICT

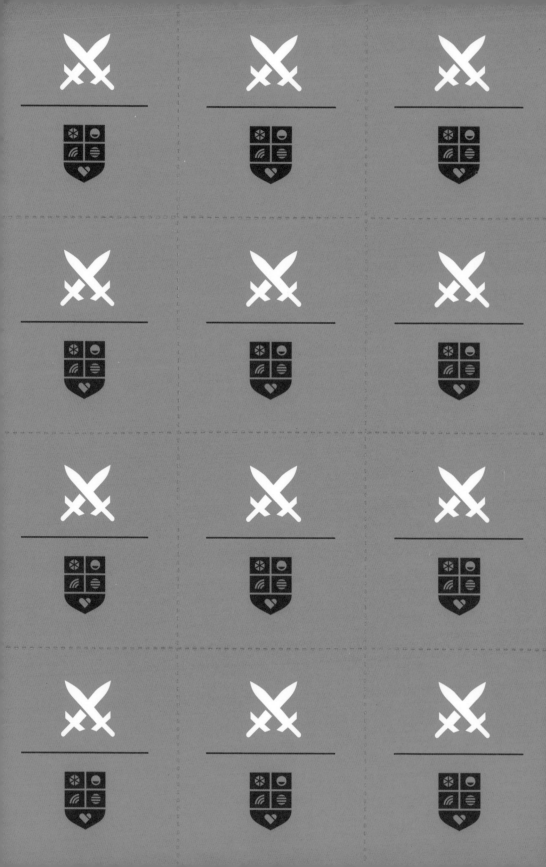

Story Cards

Did you come up with a really good one?
Jot it down, so you remember it!

Favorite story

Title:

The End.

Title:
....

....

....

....

....

....

....

....

....

.... **The End**

tle:
....

....

....

....

....

....

....

....

....

....

....

.... **The End.**

....

What's happening here?

Fill in what the characters are saying or thinking.

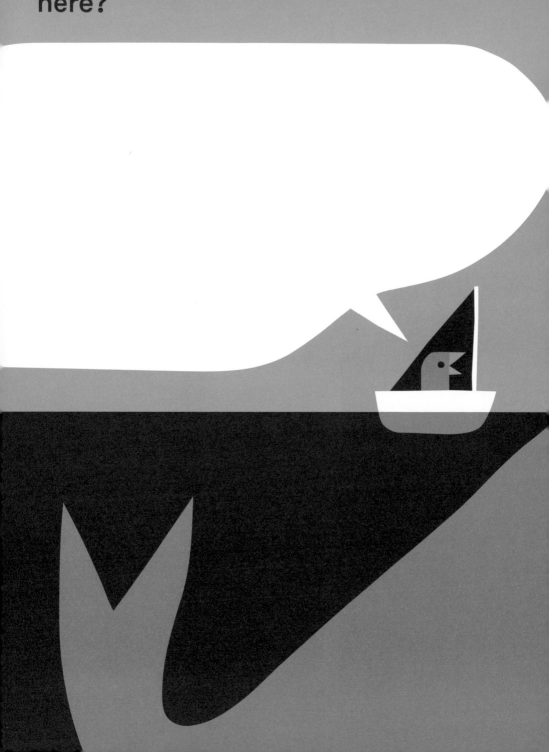

Write a story based on this picture.

....

....

....

....

....

....

....

Some things to think about:

Where is this?

Who is this?

What happened?

Do they end up OK?

Write a story based on this picture.

Title:

....

....

....

....

....

....

The End.

Poetry is a way to express feelings and ideas.

You can use language to paint a picture. **Write a poem about a bird who lost its voice.**

Title:

Do you haiku?

A haiku is a poem with just three lines. The first line has 5 syllables, the second line has 7 syllables, and the third line has 5 syllables.

Write a haiku about your socks.

Title:

5 syllables

7 syllables

5 syllables

Write a haiku about your favorite animal.

Title:

5 syllables

7 syllables

5 syllables

Write a haiku about a flower.

Title:

....
5 syllables

....
7 syllables

....
5 syllables

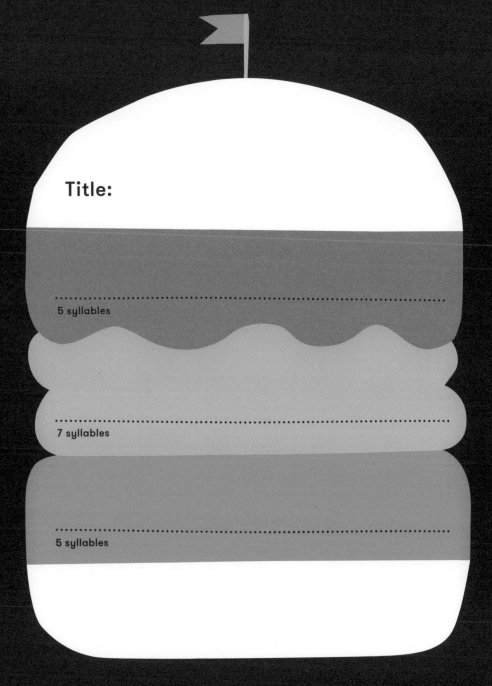

Title:

5 syllables

7 syllables

5 syllables

A haiku about a sandwich?
Why not?!

Write a poem about a superhero with an incredibly odd superpower.

superhero's name:

superpower:

Title:

....

....

....

....

....

....

....

....

....

....

....

....

Creating Comics

Comics tell stories using words and pictures.

The story is broken up into panels—with each panel showing a moment in time.

Caption boxes are used to narrate the story, guiding the reader along.

Thought bubbles tell you what the characters are thin

Speech bubbles show what the characters are saying.

Comics use words like POW, SPLAT, & KABOOM for sound effects (or SFX in comic lingo).

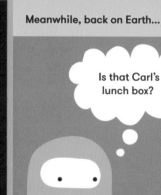

Finish this comic by filling in the
thought bubbles, speech bubbles, and SFX.

ike all good stories, a comic has a beginning, where you introduce the haracters and setting, and something interesting starts happening; a iddle, where there's a conflict or something unexpected happens; and n ending, where the conflict is resolved—whether it's happy or not is p to you! Jot down your ideas before you start filling in your panels.

Title:

Characters:

Setting:

Conflict:

Then this happens:

How the conflict is resolved:

On the next page

Based on your notes, start filling in the panels using a pencil. Once you're happy with it, you can trace over the pencil with black ink, erase your pencil lines, and add any color or shading.

Title:

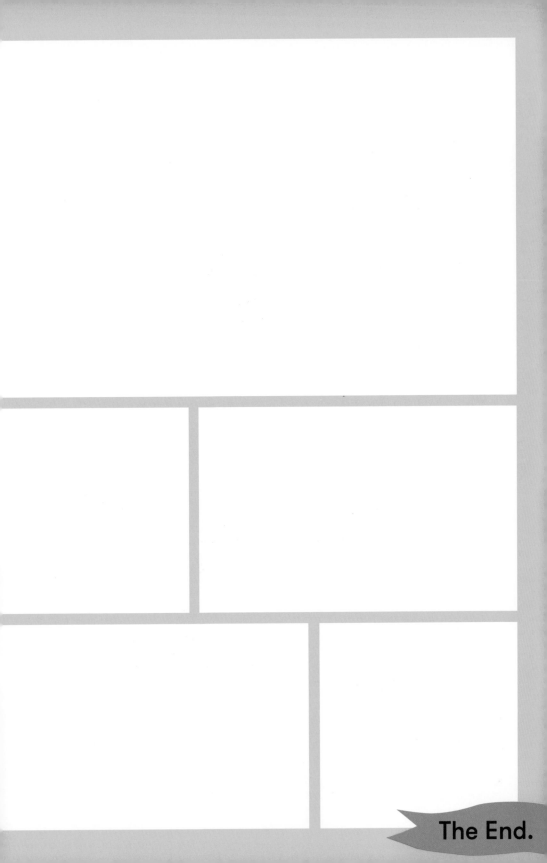

The End.

Sing It to Me

Songs tell stories with words that are set to music.
If you look at song lyrics written on paper,
they read like poetry.

ing the tune "Twinkle, Twinkle, tle Star," write your own lyrics. ur song could be about anything— three-eyed monster, a pool party, icorns. After you write it, sing it!

Title: ....

It Takes Two

Grab a writing partner! When you come up with a story together, it might go places you never expected.

1 Play one round of rock, paper, scissors. Winner decides who goes first.

2 Take turns writing sentences until you finish a story based on this illustration.

(Make sure there's a clear beginning, middle, and end!)

Title: ....

....

....

....

....

....

Cave Story

In prehistoric times, early humans created cave paintings to tell stories. Translate this cave painting into a story.

Title: ....

....

....

....

....

....

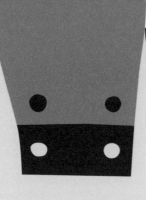

Tell a Tall Tale

A tall tale is a story with descriptions that are so exaggerated, it's unbelievable (and funny). A famous tall tale is about Paul Bunyan, a giant lumberjack and his sidekick, Babe the Blue Ox. According to legend, their footprints created the 10,000 lakes of Minnesota—and by pulling his ax behind him, Paul created the Grand Canyon. His hotcake griddle was so big, loggers greased it by skating on it with bacon sides attached to their boots.

Make up your own tall tale about Paul and Babe.

itle:

....

....

....

....

....

....

....

....

....

Have you ever heard someone give a speech? They often use stories. Pretend you're running for president. What would you tell voters?

When I am president...

....

....

....

....

....

....

Draw yourself behind the podium. ▶

"Land, ho!"

commanded Penelope the pirate, as she peered through her spyglass.

....

....

....

....

....

....

....

Some useful pirate words and phrases:

Ahoy, matey:
Hello, friend

All hands on deck!:
An urgent request for
all crew to come to
the deck to help

Argh!:
Argh!

Aye!:
Yes, or I agree

Booty:
Pirate's treasure

Buccaneer:
Pirate

Jolly Roger:
The pirate flag with a
skull and crossbones

Land, ho!:
An exclamation to use
when you first spot
land while at sea

Landlubber:
Someone who's not
very skilled at sea

Poop deck:
Deck that's the farthest
back and highest

Scuttle:
To sink a ship

Illustrate an important scene.

The End.

Dear Diary,

Keeping a diary is a great way to capture events that could become bigger stories later. Try it for a week. Spend a few minutes jotting down what happened to you each day. (Leave out the boring stuff.)

Date:

Dear Diary, ...

....

....

....

Date:

Dear Diary, ...

....

....

....

Date:

Dear Diary, ...

....

....

Date: ....

Dear Diary, ...

....

....

....

Date: ....

Dear Diary, ...

....

....

....

Date: ....

Dear Diary, ...

....

....

....

Date: ....

Dear Diary, ...

....

....

....

True Story

Some of the best stories come from your own experiences. Write about something that actually happened to you— when there was an issue that was resolved.

Before you start writing, plan your story:

When it happened .... Where you were ....

Who was there ....

....

What happened first (and what you did) ....

....

What happened next ....

....

How you felt ....

....

How it ended ....

....

BASED ON TRUE EVENTS

SOME NAMES MAY HAVE BEEN CHANGED TO PROTECT THE INNOCENT

Illustrate an important scene.

The End.

A Letter to Me

Write a letter to yourself. Only you will know if the story you tell is true or imaginary.

Dear Me,

When I woke up today, I ....

....

And then something strange happened...

....

....

....

And then ....

....

Finally, I ....

....

Can you believe it!?

Later, alligator—

Me

My Secret Code

Can you write in code? Make a unique symbol for each letter of the alphabet. Then cut out this page, and use it to write your TOP SECRET story inside the book jacket. Be sure to hide your code if you don't want anyone to figure out what your story is about.

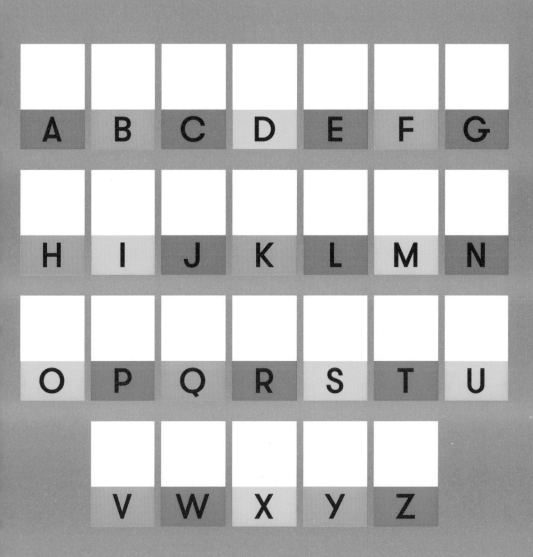

Another Secret Code

A B C D E F G

H I J K L M N

O P Q R S T U

V W X Y Z

My Story Ideas

Story ideas can come to you at any time—sparked by a crazy daydream, or someone fascinating you meet, or something weird that you see. Be sure to jot your ideas down so you have them handy when you're ready to write.

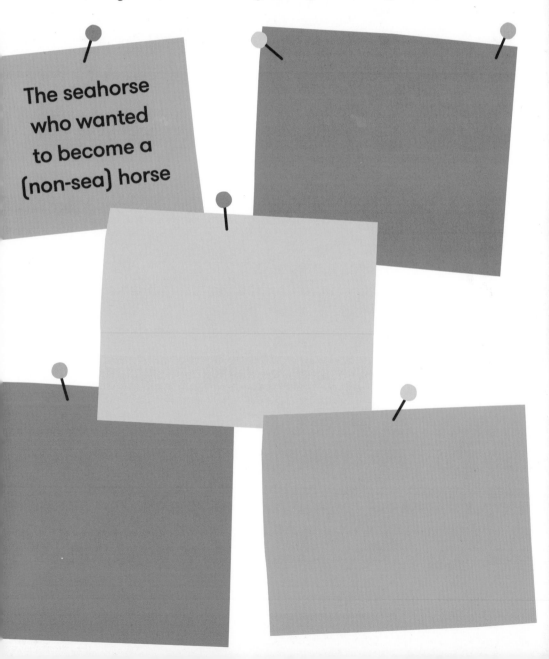

The seahorse who wanted to become a (non-sea) horse

A good storyteller is a voracious reader.

(that means super-eager)

Book Review Bookpla

Review your latest
reads on these stickers
then stick them inside
the covers of the books

My all-time favorite books
(so far)

1 ....
....

2 ....
....

3 ....
....

4 ....
....

5 ....
....

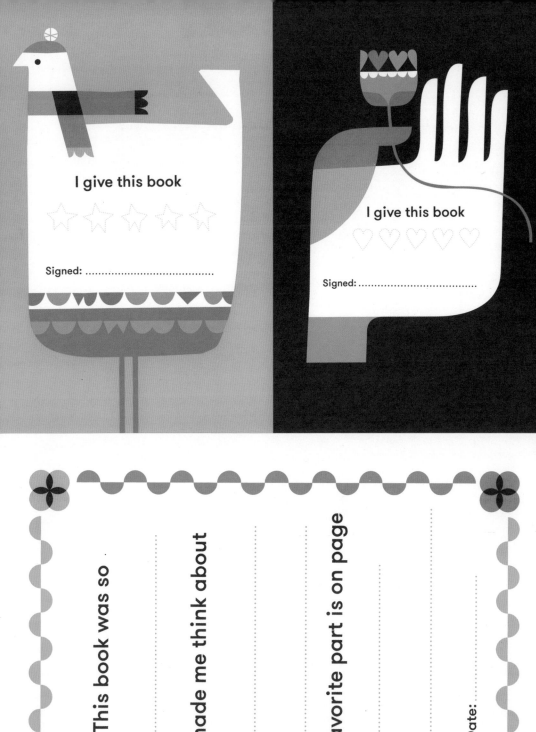

I give this book

Signed: ....

I give this book

Signed: ....

This book was so ....

It made me think about ....

My favorite part is on page ....

Signed: ....

Date: ....

Find yourself using the same words over and over?
Come up with alternatives. (Check a thesaurus for help.)

I give this book

♡ ♡ ♡ ♡ ♡

Signed: ....

I give this book

♡ ♡ ♡ ♡ ♡

Signed:

This book makes me feel
(circle one)

happy　sad　surprised　silly

bored　excited

other:..................

I'd recommend it
to a friend

☐ absolutely　☐ no way

☐ let me think about it

Signed: ....

Date: ....

When you come across an interesting, new-to-you word, jot it down.

brouhaha—an uproar or big event

catawampus—something askew or not lined up correctly; diagonal

lollygag—to waste time, mess around, or procrastinate

This is the cover of the book
I'm going to write someday.

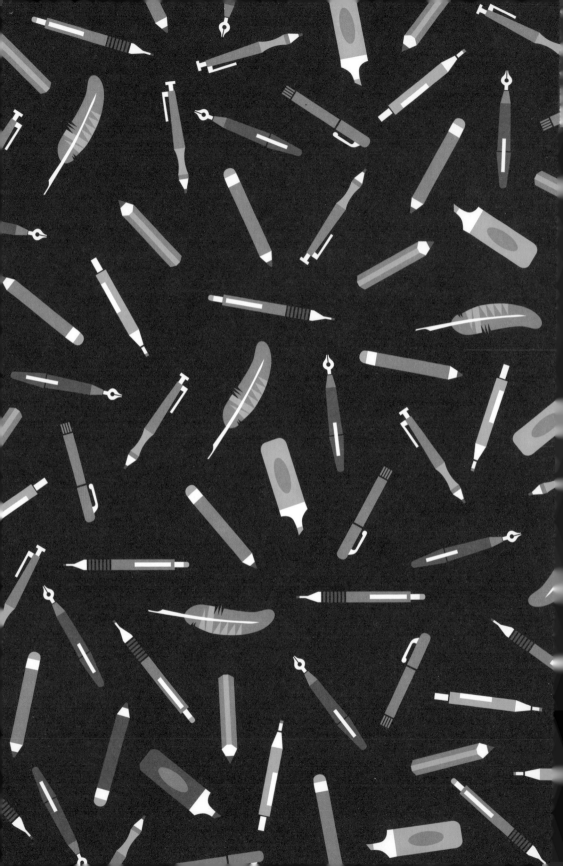